WHEN DID WOMEN START TO VOTE?

Civil Rights Books for Children

Children's History Books

Speedy Publishing LLC
40 E. Main St. #1156
Newark, DE 19711
www.speedypublishing.com

Women did not always enjoy the right to vote and hold office. Thanks to women like Susan B. Anthony and Elizabeth Cady Stanton, women, as well as people of any ethnicity, now enjoy these rights. Lucy Stone, Julia Ward Howe, and Henry Blackwell were also involved in this major accomplishment.

While our Constitution did not prohibit them from voting, it did not provide that guarantee. States had the ability to decide this issue until the 19th Amendment was ratified in 1920. Believe it or not, it was the states of the Wild West that first provided women with this right, not the "progressive" states of the East Coast and New England.

VOTE

WOMEN'S SUFFRAGE

Women's Suffrage means the women have voting rights as well as being able to hold office.

Only men were allowed to vote until the 1900s in many democracies, including early British democracies, the Roman Republic, and Ancient Greece, as well as the United States.

Until the 19th amendment was passed in 1920 in the U.S., they were not allowed to vote. This occurred much later in some countries, like Kuwait, where they did not get this right until 2005.

Some countries approved of these rights earlier, such as New Zealand, where women's suffrage was pioneered in 1893.

Register
to
Vote!

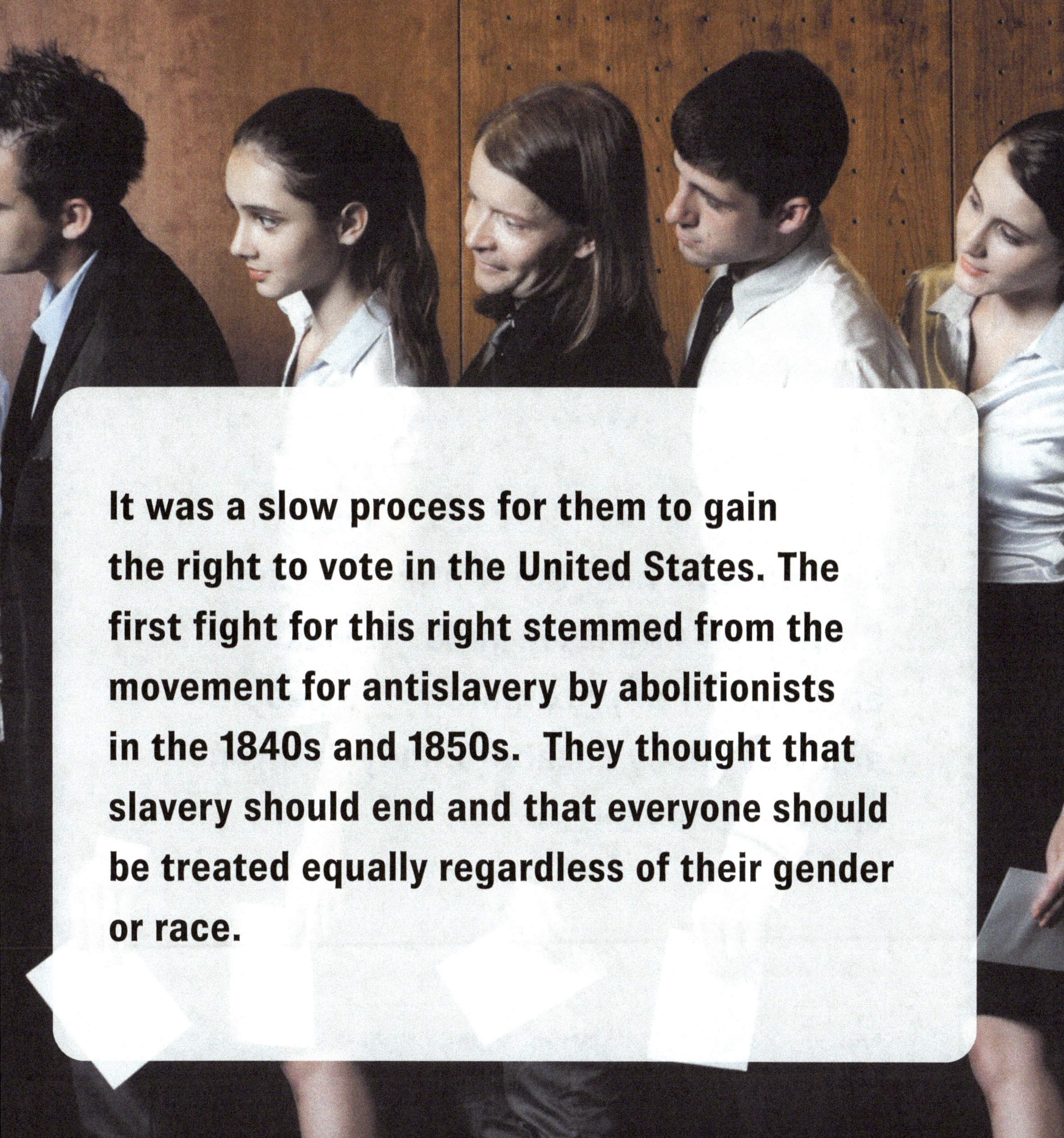

It was a slow process for them to gain the right to vote in the United States. The first fight for this right stemmed from the movement for antislavery by abolitionists in the 1840s and 1850s. They thought that slavery should end and that everyone should be treated equally regardless of their gender or race.

SENECA FALLS

Seneca Falls held the first convention for women's rights in 1848. It was attended by approximately 300 people and was led by Elizabeth Cady Stanton and Lucretia Mott.

NEW YORK
FIRST CONVENTION FOR
WOMAN'S RIGHTS
WAS HELD ON THIS CORNER
1848
STATE EDUCATION
DEPARTMENT 1932

The main objective of this convention consisted of a document similar to our Declaration of Independence, but was called "Declaration of Sentiments". This document stated that women have the same rights as men, including voting privileges.

THE SENECA FALLS CONVENTION OF 1848

The Seneca Falls Convention marked the beginning of the revolution for women's equality in America.

An educated lady from Boston named Lucretia Mott became one of the first to speak boldly regarding the rights of slaves and women. She went on tours and created pamphlets, alongside Elizabeth Cady Stanton and Susan B. Anthony, demanding they all be treated fairly.

NATIONAL WOMEN'S SUFFRAGE ASSOCIATION

In 1869 the National Women's Suffrage Association was formed by leaders Susan B. Anthony and Elizabeth Cady Stanton. Their main objective was to pass an amendment that gave them voting rights.

MASS MEETING
VOTES
FOR
WOMEN

V
O

They wanted this right, as well as for all ethnicities, to be included in the 15th amendment. It passed in 1870 but only allowing men of all races to vote, not including women. The American Woman Suffrage Association was created in 1869.

It's leaders were Julia Ward Howe, Lucy Stone, and Henry Blackwell. These groups could not agree in supporting the 15th amendment.

They then merged in 1894 under Susan B. Anthony's leadership and became known as the National Woman Suffrage Association. This Association's priority was passing the 19th amendment.

Although the government did not provide them with voting privileges, they starting making progress in some territories and state. They were given voting privileges in the Wyoming Territory in 1869.

Then, in 1869, Wyoming agreed to become a part of the Union only if they gave women the right to vote. Colorado was the first state to grant women the right to vote by adopting an amendment in 1893.

It wasn't long before more western states stared to amend their constitutions and this got the momentum going in the early 1900s.

THE 19TH AMENDMENT

This amendment guarantees that they are able to vote in the United States. First introduced in 1878, it didn't become ratified until more than 41 years later on August 18,1920.

Senator Aaron Sargent out of California introduced this amendment in 1878. He strongly believed that women should be able to vote. It remained stuck in the Senate for nine years and was finally voted on in 1887. The Senate rejected it by a vote of 16 to 34.

While momentum to pass the amendment stopped for several years, in the early 1900s Congress again took a look at it. In 1918, it passed the House of Representatives but not the Senate.

In the early part of 1919, the Senate again voted, but failed to pass it by one vote. Originally against the amendment, President Wilson then held a special session in the Spring of 1919 and asked them to pass it. The Senate finally passed it on June 4, 1919.

This amendment was ratified quickly since several states had already allowed women to vote. Thirty-five states ratified it by March of 1920. In order to meet the requirements of the Constitution, one more state was required. Many states had rejected it as well and the final decision fell onto Tennessee. At first it appeared that the Tennessee legislature decision was a tie.

Representative Burn then changed his vote and voted in agreement of the amendment. While he was originally against this amendment, he announced later that he was convinced by his mother to vote in favor of it. The first time that all women were able to vote was held in November of 1920 and millions of women of all ages voted.

For Better Living
ROOSEVELT
LEARN
TO VOTE

SUSAN B. ANTHONY

Susan B. Anthony was a leader for women's rights born on February 15, 1820 in Massachusetts. Her middle name was Brownell. She was one of six sisters and brothers, and some of them were also involved.

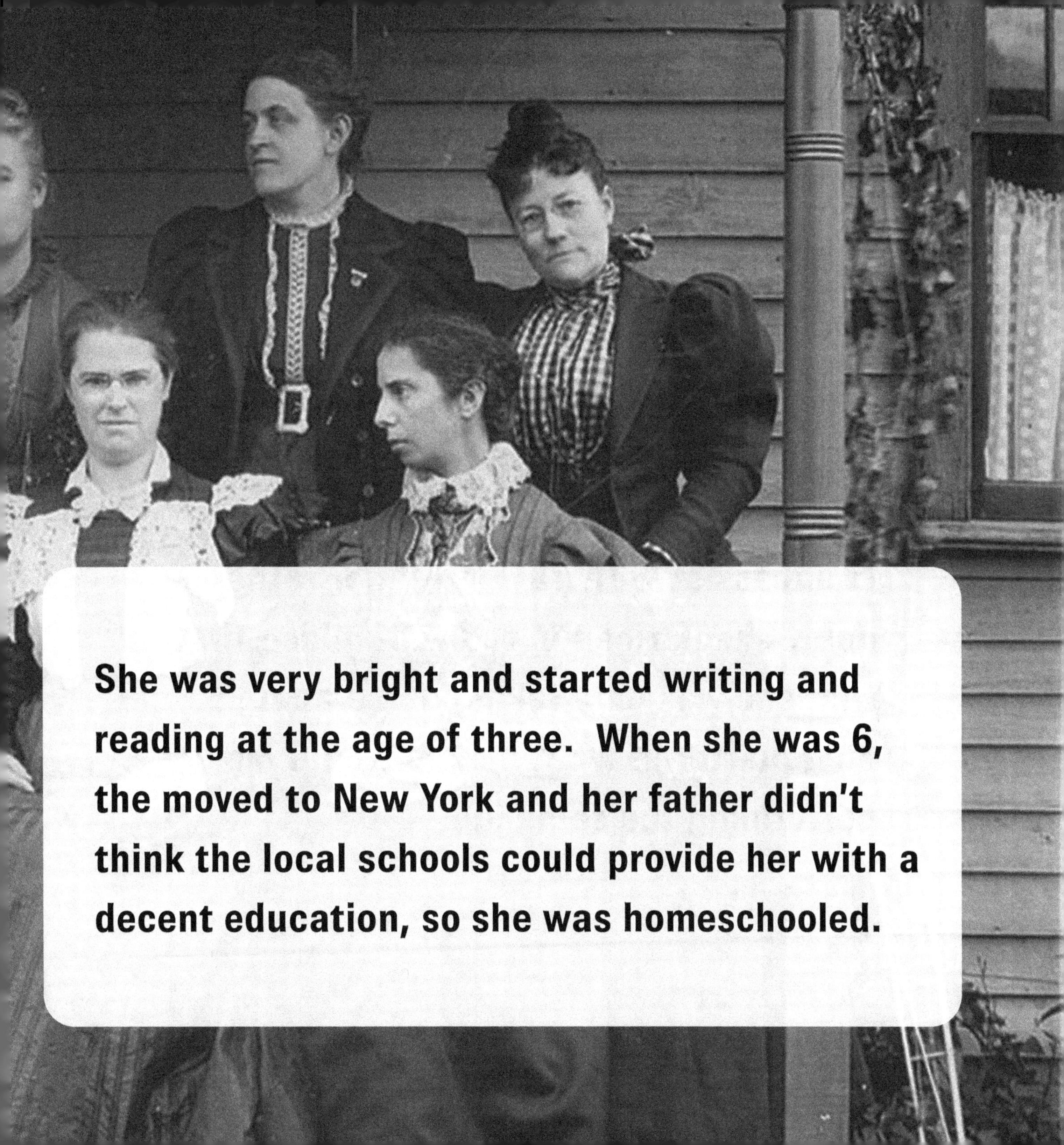

She was very bright and started writing and reading at the age of three. When she was 6, the moved to New York and her father didn't think the local schools could provide her with a decent education, so she was homeschooled.

Life got difficult for her and her family when in 1837 the economy collapsed and her father lost most of his belongings. She then began teaching so that she could assist with paying off her father's debt. She noticed in the work place first that she was only taking home about one-quarter of what a male would make performing the same job.

OUR RIGHT TO VOTE!
E!
WOMEN'S RIGHTS!

This didn't appear to be right to her. That is when she got involved in getting laws enacted that said that men and women should have equal rights. In continuance of her fight, she illegally voted in the 1872 elections and was fined $100. She refused to pay this fine. This was only the beginning of her struggle to obtain the rights for women to vote.

At one time there was a coin in her honor named the Susan B. Anthony Dollar. It was similar in size to the quarter, but was worth one dollar. The Susan B. Anthony museum is the house that she was born in and opened its doors in 2010.

ELIZABETH CADY STANTON

Elizabeth Cady was born in a family of 10 sisters and brothers in Johnstown, New York on November 12, 1815. Unfortunately, several of them perished at a young age. Elizabeth and four sisters were the only children to live into adulthood. Eleazar, her remaining brother, died at 20 which left her mother in a depressed state of mind and Elizabeth knowing that her father wanted her to be a boy.

While growing up, she became to know the law by her father Daniel. He became a lawyer and also a judge and U.S. Congressman. She soon learned that it was not the same for women and men and that only men had the right to vote and women had very few rights. She felt this was unfair and felt that she was as smart as any man and therefore should have the same rights.

Elizabeth wanted to attend college after high school but soon learned that women were not accepted at major universities. She then ended up attending a girls' college and was able to continue with her studies. She soon started believing strongly in individual rights regardless of their gender or race. She married Henry Stanton, an abolitionist, in 1840.

They had seven children. She continued to work on improving these rights over the next 30 years. Unfortunately, she did not live long enough to see the result of her hard work.

In a speech titled The Solitude of Self, she talked about in front of the United States Congress about the rights of women. She is also known for the phrase "the history of the past is but one long struggle upward to equality."

The USS Elizabeth C. Stanton is a World War II battleship named for her and her home in Seneca Falls has been proclaimed a National Historic Landmark.

For more information about Women's Suffrage, check out your local library, research the internet, and ask questions of your teachers, family, and friends.

Visit

BABY PROFESSOR
EDUCATION KIDS

www.BabyProfessorBooks.com

to download Free Baby Professor eBooks and view our catalog of new and exciting Children's Books

www.ingramcontent.com/pod-product-compliance
Lightning Source LLC
LaVergne TN
LVHW060508170826
845677LV00026B/1647
* 9 7 9 8 8 6 9 4 3 0 0 2 1 *